Little Laureates

Poems From
North West England Vol II
Edited by Annabel Cook

First published in Great Britain in 2007 by:
Young Writers
Remus House
Coltsfoot Drive
Peterborough
PE2 9JX
Telephone: 01733 890066
Website: www.youngwriters.co.uk

SB ISBN 978-1 84431 218 4

Foreword

Young Writers was established in 1991 and has been passionately devoted to the promotion of reading and writing in children and young adults ever since. The quest continues today. Young Writers remains as committed to the nurturing of poetic and literary talent as ever.

This year's Young Writers competition has proven as vibrant and dynamic as ever and we are delighted to present a showcase of the best poetry from across the UK and in some cases overseas. Each poem has been selected from a wealth of *Little Laureates* entries before ultimately being published in this, our sixteenth primary school poetry series.

Once again, we have been supremely impressed by the overall quality of the entries we have received. The imagination, energy and creativity which has gone into each young writer's entry made choosing the poems a challenging and often difficult but ultimately hugely rewarding task - the general high standard of the work submitted ensured this opportunity to bring their poetry to a larger appreciative audience.

We sincerely hope you are pleased with this final collection and that you will enjoy *Little Laureates Poems From North West England Vol II* for many years to come.

08809

THIS ITEM MUST BE RETURNED OR RENEWED ON OR BEFORE THE LATEST DATE SHOWN

EDDA COMMUNITY LIBRARY
Monday - Friday 10.00am - 4.00pm
Saturday 10.00am - 1.00pm
Tel: 01704 578003 · Email: eddaarts@btconnect.com
Part of the Bridge Inn Community Farm Ltd.

Contents

Green Park Community Primary & Nursery School, Maghull

Josh Jackson (9)	37
Daniel Halford (9)	38
Ellie Edwards (10)	39
Thomas Dickson (10)	40
Jack Thomas Cunnah (9)	41
Chloe Coughlin (10)	42
Megan Calleja (10)	43
Molly Shields (10)	44
Bethany Ryan (10)	45
Anneli Reed (10)	46
Sean Reddock (10)	47
Melissa Perrin (10)	48
Emily McLean (9)	49
Jack McGregor (10)	50
Kyle Lewis (10)	51
Michael Johnson (10)	52
Milly Brady (9)	53
Connor Boswarva (10)	54
Emma Bullen (9)	55
Emily Bateman (10)	56
Matthew Albertina (10)	57
Sam Albanese (10)	58
Holly Hunter (10)	59
Sian Williams (9)	60
Brooke Whittle (10)	61
George Walsh (9)	62

Higham St John's CE (Controlled) Primary School, Higham

Isabel Warren (7)	63
Joel Punchard (9)	64
Molly Louise Barnes (8)	65
Alex Boland (8)	66
Harry Jackson-Smith (7)	67
Ben Cox	68
Callam Barnes (8)	69
Daniel Shapland (8)	70
Kezia Brown (8)	71
Andrew Danson (8)	72
Poppie Brogan (8)	73
Olivia Forrest (8)	74

Bethany Gregson (8)   75
Connor Quinn (8)   76
Jacob Ratcliffe (7)   77
Cameron Walby (8)   78
Jake McNair   79
Emily Pickup (8)   80
Ben Jenkinson (8)   81
Victoria Parr (9)   82
Jenny Plunkett (8)   83
Bradley Jones (8)   84
Thomas Stinchon (8)   85
Ryan Moir (8)   86
Simra Ud-Din (8)   87
Georgia Mackay   88

Maryport CE Junior School, Maryport

Hayley Sarah Roberts (11)   89
Hannah Pattinson (11)   90
Heather-Leigh Fox (11)   91
Ashton Hunton (10)   92
Thomas Graham (11)   93
Jane Telford (11)   94
Alec Telfer (10)   95
Ellie Tunstall (11)   96
Sean Brough (10)   97
Carrie Brogden (11)   98
Ashlea Hill (11)   99
Hannah Bethwaite (11)   100
Charlie Donaldson (10)   101
Adam Wozencroft (11)   102
Emily Ford (11)   103
Hayden Barcock (10)   104
Callum James Morley (10)   105
Antonia Hodgson (11)   106
Dylan Renac (10)   107
Daniel Hutchinson (11)   108

St Mary's RC Primary & Nursery School, Langley

Lauren Thomas (8)   109
Paul Navin (7)   110
Chelsea-Lee Stone (8)   111

St Vincent's RC Primary School, Penketh

Hannah Shaw (11)	153
Tara Moran (11)	154
Jennifer Gibbons (11)	155
Ben Baxter (11)	156
Zachary Wilde (10)	157
Aamil Ashraf (10)	158
Emily Purcell (11)	159
Charlie English (11)	160
Daniel McCormick (11)	161
Hannah Rhodes (10)	162
Amy Matthews (11)	163
Meghan Gleave (11)	164
Claudia Perez (11)	165
Kendell Redmond (11)	166
Beth Carrington (11)	167
Jennifer Campbell (11)	168
Joseph Ellison (11)	169
Alex Preston (10)	170

Sutton Green Primary School, Little Sutton

Charlotte Parry (8)	171
Daniel McCabe (9)	172
Victoria Garner (7)	173
Philip Jones (9)	174
Imogen Buckley (9)	175
Emmy Byrnes (9)	176
Darren Whitehill (8)	177
Jessica Doig (8)	178
Robbie Rogers (9)	179
Owen Rutter (8)	180
Deanna Fairhurst (9)	181
Alex Cranston (9)	182
Sophie Quinn (8)	183
Holly Powell (9)	184
Lydia Proctor (9)	185

The Poems

The Wonderful World Of The Beach

Driftwood on the ground,
That lies there never to be found.
Crashing waves on the shore,
Pushing shells up more and more.

Dalmatians playing in the sand,
While their owners are listening to a band.
All the people going home,
Past the car park into the unknown.

Anthony Fairlamb (10)
Brampton Junior School, Brampton

Puppies

Woof, woof goes the dog's litter,
As they run around, getting fitter.
Their paws pattering on the ground,
As they run round and round.
Max, Lucky and the rest
Really think this is the best.

Chasing their tails all day long,
Then the mother sees something wrong,
Their food bowl is empty,
But the cupboard has plenty.
The puppies finally get their lunch
And then they sleep in a bunch.

Thomas McGaffin (10)
Brampton Junior School, Brampton

The Fashion Queen

Shoes, shoes, what beautiful shoes,
Oh how they look so nice
There's boots, sandals and high heels
And much more, that I like.
But then when I was making trends,
I found out I had split ends,
I ran out of school just to look cool and
Then I fell into a pool.

Leanne Woods (11)
Brampton Junior School, Brampton

Music

Bashing, crashing, thumping, banging,
Cymbals loud and always clanging.
Drums being hit and making loud sounds,
Organs being played, heard all around,
Music is a wonderful thing.

Victoria Waugh (11)
Brampton Junior School, Brampton

The Chooby

The Chooby trampled over trees,
Its tummy jangled like rusty keys.
Its trail of slime led through the woods,
Its wanglets shaped like cotton buds,
The gobar, gobar on its head.
Its coloured skin as black as lead.
The poison spit comes from its wad,
The Chooby oh Chooby is really bad!
Its eyes as green as summer grass.
If you walked by, you would not pass.
It has no arms but ears, oh yes!
The Chooby, Chooby, what a mess!
Its mouth as big as two oak doors,
It likes to chew on apple cores.
So if I was you, I'd watch out,
The Chooby, Chooby is always about . . .

Shannon Rebecca Johnston (11)
Brampton Junior School, Brampton

The Hungry Eskimo

Bump went the Eskimo's tummy
I think my stomach has gone funny
No one knows just how
I could eat a fish or a cow
With two hundred and twenty-two fish and chips
And seven thousand juicy dips
Anyone could fill their big fat lips
With sweets, hot dogs and five hundred round crisps
It seems that I could cover the nation
Because this is only my imagination.

Gemma Peascod (11)
Brampton Junior School, Brampton

Crazy

I live in a strange place - it's not quite so ordinary,
It's sort of like the same place, in cartoons you see on telly.
It doesn't make much sense to me, so it won't to you at all,
But there's one thing I can tell you
I just know you'll love it all . . .
The queen runs round in underwear and the prince,
He's just as bad, but I suppose that's actually normal, cos
My whole world's completely mad!
There's clouds made of candyfloss and fish that fly behind,
And there's pigs swimming in the river cos
I live inside my mind!

Daniella Jade Ansell (11)
Brampton Junior School, Brampton

Motocross

M otocross is a muddy sport
O ver the jumps and into the air
T able tops are the names of some jumps
O bserve the riders
C anadians do a lot of motocross
R aces are very long
O nly one rider wins
S oily tracks
S andy tracks.

Owen Potts (11)
Brampton Junior School, Brampton

Ugh! I Hate It

Ugh, I hate it when she is like this,
She makes me do ballet
But I told her, ballet is not for boys
It's for tiny girls that always get their own way!

Ugh! I hate it when he is like this,
He made me wash his car
I told him it isn't for little boys
It's for grown-ups, not moi!

Yes, I love it when they're like this
Not making me do anything
It's a joy to sit down all day
On TV I could watch the opera sing!

Emily Black (11)
Brampton Junior School, Brampton

Why No Homework?

Monday's work was stolen by an eagle,
Flying in a clear blue sky,
I tried to get it, yes I did
But the eagle was just too high.

Tuesday's work was taken
By a tiny robot Mip,
It found my work interesting,
So it took it to its ship.

Wednesday's work was eaten
By a hungry black dog.
It had three heads, I couldn't stop it
So it ran off into the fog.

Thursday's work was burnt
By a scaly dragon's flame,
It went all black and crunchy
It's the dragon that should get the blame.

I didn't bother bringing Friday's work,
It's as simple as can be,
There is a reason I didn't bring it,
The author was a chimpanzee.

Alex Stockwell (11)
Brampton Junior School, Brampton

Forest

The wind blew harshly in my ears,
And the tall trees sway,
I saw a large spider, that's one of my fears
I wish I were away.

The golden leaves crackled beneath my feet
The sea-blue sky,
The dew covered the grass, like a sheet,
And I wondered why?

The tree's shadows trapped me in
Blueberry bushes.
I tripped on a rock and hurt my shin,
And the mud mushes.

The birds were singing in the treetops,
Creepers on trees.
The trees watched over me like cops,
The strong breeze.

Sophie Murray (10)
Brampton Junior School, Brampton

Summer

S unshine, morning and night
U nlimited time to play outside,
M y family's favourite season; everything so bright,
M y favourite place is at the seaside.
E verybody looking happy in their gardens,
R ays of sunlight beaming down on them.

Charlotte Graham (11)
Brampton Junior School, Brampton

Through The Jungle

On my journey through the jungle . . .
There were slimy slithery snakes, wrapped around
The branches in the trees, they were very
Scary, so I carried on with my journey.

On my journey through the jungle . . .
The tigers and lions, fighting over a bit of meat
On the treetops, so I stepped out of the way
And carried on my journey.

On my journey through the jungle . . .
There were rhinos splashing in the mud pool.
I ran so I didn't get muddy and that was all,
On my journey through the jungle!

Rebecca Stoddart (11)
Brampton Junior School, Brampton

Stable Fever

I must go down to the stable again to see
the big black horse,
And all I ask is a brand new jump to put
on the obstacle course.
And the horse will kick and I will fall off
and land on the muddy floor!
The horse will walk and walk and walk
straight through the big wooden door.

I must go down to the stable again to make
a new obstacle course,
I will run out of the door and
into the field and climb up on to my horse,
And all I ask is a new horse and field
for I am a champion with a shield.

Sarah Clapperton (11)
Brampton Junior School, Brampton

Friends

Friends can be nice, friends can be mean,
But there's no one like my best friend Ashleigh.
She's always there, when I'm happy and sad,
She's always there to make me feel glad.

We do everything together,
Through sun and rain.
When I'm not feeling so good
She will hug me again.

On birthdays we share,
We always care.
We draw each other pictures with pens,
Because we're the best of friends.

Karis Stockwell (11)
Brampton Junior School, Brampton

Angels Of Love

Your love will never die for him,
You'll always have your dreams.
Remember all the good times
You had throughout the years.
You'll smile for him
You'll cry for him
You'll even laugh out loud.
Then you'll remember things he did,
That really made you proud,
But even though the angels
Came and took your son away,
He's watching down upon you
Each and every day.

Jodi Deeney (11)
Brampton Junior School, Brampton

My Dog!

My dog got out of the garden
and ran down our town road.
He boarded a plane, that took him to Spain
and he ran all the way back home.

My dog got out of the garden,
and went to my auntie Peggy's.
He grabbed her comb and brought it home
then ate one of my teddies.

My dog got out of the garden
but I was ready for him,
I threw the net
and he hurt his leg.
So now he's at the vet.

I've padlocked the gate in my garden
so now he can't get out.
He's tried and tried
he's cried and cried
cos he can't get out the garden.

Amy Farish (11)
Brampton Junior School, Brampton

The Game Of Football

Football is the greatest game,
playing professional gets you fame.

Running past defenders with the wind in your face,
being a striker you need pace.

Mid-fielders set up the goals galore
making strikers score, more and more.

Being a defender you stop the strikers
scoring, making the match very boring.

Being a keeper, you stop the goals
diving for the ball at strikers' toes.

Jonathan Winthrop (11)
Brampton Junior School, Brampton

Part V; The Lady Of Shallot

As the loose boat drifted past,
Everyone saw her real at last,
Sir Lancelot looked on aghast,
Then fled away, very fast.
                    The Lady of Shallot.

While the fleeing Lancelot,
Charged past a village, he forgot
That's what he had sadly done,
Was marked on him, whatever he won.
                    The Lover of Shallot.

As he rode down the narrow track,
He thought; *as a knight, I've got the sack,*
The armour shone; though it was black,
'No sword can pass - it would crack,'
                    Said Sir Lancelot.

Sir Lancelot at last turned round,
And looked sadly at the ground,
Then dismounted and painfully found
His neck was broken, clean and sound.
                    'Oh no!' cried Sir Lancelot.

Alex Westerberg (11)
Brampton Junior School, Brampton

Pirates

Pirates, pirates, big and round,
If they fall they'll bounce off the ground!

A brand new pirate flag wafting in the air,
When all of a sudden, it starts to tear.

Big black cannons blasting away,
Well that put an end to that nice day!

The pirates set off and sailed away.
An hour later, they had been put astray.

Suddenly the pirates found a pink pearl,
The whole crew started screaming like a girl.

Ellen Reed (11)
Brampton Junior School, Brampton

My Little Sister, Hayley!

Monday; she caught it by the feathers,
Poor duck, now she's wrestled it and started to pluck.

Tuesday; oh for the love of God, she placed herself
In the flower bed, eating peas in a pod!

Wednesday; curse thee, thou foul Yeti, she's
Shredded my homework into confetti!

Thursday; I look in my mirror as I'm doing my hair,
Poof! Out Hayley came from the depths of her lair.

Friday; for Pete's sake (our Dad) it's getting worse,
Now she starts to devour my favourite purse!

Charlotte Smith (11)
Brampton Junior School, Brampton

Date Plan

Buying, spending in the shops,
Eating giant lollipops.
New Look is the place to go,
Then off to a fashion show.
Getting pampered, like a teen
Now I look a drama queen,
So many shoes, which ones to pick?
Ready for my date with Rick.
Candlelit dinner by the sea,
Then he gives me his house key.
After a hard day of shopping and a date,
I go to bed, nearly awake.

Hayley Waugh (10)
Brampton Junior School, Brampton

Dragons

In the land of the dragons . . .
Where reptiles roam like wagons,
And hill giants colonise in groups,
In the Marinas Jungle, vines hang in loops.

In the land of the dragons . . .
Where reptiles roam like wagons,
And goblins raid small towns,
Stumbling round pubs, like clowns.

In the land of the dragons . . .
Where reptiles roam like wagons,
And in some caves drinking beer in flagons
Live the dragons!

Samuel Bancroft (11)
Brampton Junior School, Brampton

What Is Anger?

Anger is a fire burning deep down inside you
Waiting to jump out and *shout!*

Anger sounds like a really, really loud gun
Which has been shot.

Anger tastes like a red-hot pepper
Burning in your mouth!

Anger smells of smoke, darkening in the sky
Then fading away.

It feels like lightning, electrocuting me.
It makes me throw my covers at my brother.

Joseph Jones (9)
Bowness CP School, Little Lever

Anger Is Dark Blue

Anger is fire exploding,
Anger sounds like thunder and lightning,
Bombing all on Bonfire day.

It tastes like fire exploding in your heart,
Anger smells like blood.
It looks like people fighting each other.

Anger feels like when you shouldn't be there,
It reminds you of fighting in World War 1
And World War II.

Kane Nowell (7) & Sachin Patel (8)
Bowness CP School, Little Lever

Love Is Lavender

Love is pink clouds, chocolate watering in your mouth,
Roses coming from the sky, filling the air.
Love sounds like a rose playing a harp,
Whispers of romance, echoes of love.

Sarah Davies (8)
Bowness CP School, Little Lever

What Is Excitement?

Excitement is something that brings you happiness.
Excitement sounds like a piano playing a happy song
and somebody screaming.
Excitement tastes like something sweet and juicy.
Excitement looks like someone jumping up and down
and flapping their arms like they are going to fly.
Excitement feels like happiness and joyfulness wanting to burst out.
Excitement reminds me of I've just been born.

Katie James (9)
Bowness CP School, Little Lever

I Feel Surprised

It sounds like everyone is singing Happy Birthday
to their school friend and they're eating their meal
inside the kitchen.
It tastes of sweets and chocolate and
even yummy cheesecake.
A sandwich,
A blackcurrant juice and
Orange juice as well.

Lauren Bill (8)
Bowness CP School, Little Lever

What Is Anger?

Anger is a bomb dropping near you,
Anger tastes like hot and spicy Monster Munch.
Anger is getting arrested and being put in prison,
Anger sounds like a plane crashing.
Anger looks like all of your family in a car crash.
Anger smells like burning tyres.
Anger makes you feel like you're squashing a frog.
Anger reminds you about when someone in your family dies.

Alex Joe Eaton (9)
Bowness CP School, Little Lever

Happiness Is Red

Happiness is fun and it is sweet
It sounds like someone is screaming
And laughing on the phone
Happiness smells like roses and perfume
Mixed up together
Bins and sweets
It tastes like chocolate and roses.

Lauren Fenna
Bowness CP School, Little Lever

Excitement

Excitement sounds like laughing
And cheering from all over.

It tastes like bubbly chocolate
Custard and chocolate creamy cake.

It smells like bright colourful
Flowers reflecting in the sun.

Excitement looks like a massive
Celebration with presents.

It feels like going on holiday
For a surprise.

Excitement reminds me of my
Birthday and Christmas.

Hannah Moffat (9)
Bowness CP School, Little Lever

What Is Love?

Love is like a butterfly
Love sounds like a bird
It does not stop singing
It's like a million birds singing on a tree
Love tastes like chocolate melting down your mouth
Crunchy cherry in a sweet in your belly
Saying mmm!
Love smells like sweet sugar and perfume
In a fresh bottle.
It smells like a million roses in a garden
Love looks like a big red heart.

James Wintour & Jade Haughton (7)
Bowness CP School, Little Lever

Happiness

Happiness is cheerful and joyful,
Happiness sounds like children laughing.
Happiness tastes like chocolate cake
Melting in the chocolate custard.
Happiness smells like 1000 roses sitting under the sun,
Happiness looks like roses waving in the sun.
Happiness feels like softening on my skin.
Happiness reminds me of children
Jumping in the sky, over the sun.

Hannah Dewhurst (9)
Bowness CP School, Little Lever

Excitement

Excitement is happiness, joyful, makes you cheer up,
Excitement sounds like laughing ducks.
It tastes like Cadbury, melting, yoke coming out from the chocolate.
Excitement smells like chocolate digestives.
Excitement looks like children running around the grass.
It feels like my heart pumping,
It reminds me of children jumping up in the blazing shining sky.

Tyra Harrison (9)
Bowness CP School, Little Lever

Scary Is Black

Scary sounds like a ghost in a haunted house
with a guitar screeching loud.

Scary tastes like disgusting dirty blood,
with spiders tinkling inside you.

It looks like big towers falling
with the smell of dry dust.

You can feel your heart beeping fast,
like a drum banging you.

It reminds you of going in a graveyard at midnight,
spooky and alone.

Hakeem Ahmed & Saul Bond (8)
Bowness CP School, Little Lever

Jealousy Is Lime

Jealousy is a feeling when you want what they have
and it is a feeling that you want to snatch it off them
and you want to stamp your feet.

Natalie Herrity (8)
Bowness CP School, Little Lever

Darkness

Darkness is black, like the haze outside my house,
It smells like nothing,
It tastes like nothing
And it feels like nothing.
It reminds me of my bedroom when the light goes out,
It sounds like a scream in a dark tunnel at night.
It looks like a shadow monster, trying to get into your dreams.

Josh Jackson (9)
Green Park Community Primary & Nursery School, Maghull

Fun!

Fun is blue, like the silky Everton home kit, sparkling in the sunlight,
It sounds like the huge ground screaming in my eardrums.
It tastes like sweet sweets, melting in your mouth.
It smells like freshly baked pies and sausage rolls.
It looks like it never ends and the freshly cut grass.
It feels like the best thing in the world.
It reminds me of the huge and best
Team in the world, which is Everton!

Come on you Blues!

Daniel Halford (9)
Green Park Community Primary & Nursery School, Maghull

Laughter

Laughter is red like a shining rose,
It sounds like The Sound of Music.
It tastes like candyfloss,
It smells like flowers growing.
It looks like blossom on a tree,
Laughter feels like a soft feather on your face.
Laughter reminds me of my class.

Ellie Edwards (10)
Green Park Community Primary & Nursery School, Maghull

Frustration

Frustration is red, like a raging fire,
Sounds like a firework exploding in the deep dark sky.
It tastes like a chilli, on fire
It smells like a group of flaming ashes.
It looks like a hundred degree fireball on Earth.
Frustration feels like a fireball in my head,
Frustration reminds me of a raging fight
Somewhere by a fireball.

Thomas Dickson (10)
Green Park Community Primary & Nursery School, Maghull

Sadness

Sadness is blue like the sea washing me away,
Sadness sounds like a child sobbing when upset.
It tastes like horrible mouldy spinach.
It smells like blueberries all gone off.
Sadness looks all blue, like a bluebell.
The feel of sadness is like a hard obstacle in my way.
It reminds me of when I've been picked on
Which doesn't happen anymore.
The thing you don't want to be is sad.

Jack Thomas Cunnah (9)
Green Park Community Primary & Nursery School, Maghull

Happiness

Happiness is yellow, like golden beaches
It sounds like cheerful children laughing with their teachers
Happiness has the sweetest taste, just like candyfloss
It smells like a beautiful bunch of flowers
On a warm summer's day.
It looks like a gleaming smile coming my way
It feels like you're on top of the world,
It reminds me of the shimmering sun.
Happiness is so much fun.

Chloe Coughlin (10)
Green Park Community Primary & Nursery School, Maghull

Darkness

Darkness is black, like a black hole in space,
It sounds like a tornado ripping up the world.
Tastes as rotten as fish that's been sitting there for two days.
It smells like a tip, full of rubbish,
Looks like a hole that goes on forever.
It feels razor-sharp at the edge.
Reminds me of space with no stars, no moon and no planets.

Megan Calleja (10)
Green Park Community Primary & Nursery School, Maghull

Silence

Silence is white, like the snow falling from the glistening blue sky,
The smell is fresh and crisp, like golden vanilla ice cream.
It is peaceful, like tears running down your soft baby skin.
Silence tastes fresh, like mints rolling round your tongue.
You feel relaxed and calm, like palm trees swaying in the light breeze.
You cannot see it, but you know the sort of feeling is there.
It reminds me of blossom blowing off the trees while flowers grow
their wonderful pink petals!

Molly Shields (10)
Green Park Community Primary & Nursery School, Maghull

Laughter

Laughter is pink like a beautiful tulip, blossoming in the field,
It sounds like bluebirds singing outside my window, sitting
on the balcony.
Bubbly pink champagne and the icing on the cake.
Like perfume drifting around my head.
It looks like lots of little piglets, squeaking and rolling in the mud,
And it feels like the beautiful pink feathers of a flamingo.
It reminds me of fun, family and friends,
All together, telling jokes happily, having a great time.

Bethany Ryan (10)
Green Park Community Primary & Nursery School, Maghull

Happiness!

Happiness is light blue like the glittering sea, sparkling in the sunlight.
Waves crashing on the bay as though white horses are galloping free.
The beautiful taste is like country yoghurt sliding down,
like a green snake.
The sweet smell of salt flying so gracefully through the peaceful air.
A mass of blue and white capped mountains rolling
and crashing down.
Happiness is winning a medal as though you will never lose.
Happiness reminds me of being with friends and always laughing.
Being happy is a great thing when you're in the happy mood!

Anneli Reed (10)
Green Park Community Primary & Nursery School, Maghull

Darkness

Darkness is black like infinite space
Sounding like silence, waiting to
launch an attack.
Tasting so bitter, like a doctor's pill
It smells like evil, stalking its
unsuspecting prey
When looked at, it is nowhere to be seen
It feels so rough, like the hardest
diamond ever
Reminding me of a dark dusty alleyway
at night.
Darkness is never there . . .

Sean Reddock (10)
Green Park Community Primary & Nursery School, Maghull

Happiness

Happiness is yellow like a sour lemon,
It sounds like the roots of laughter and quiet giggles.
It feels like you can fly higher than all the birds in the world.
It looks like a beaming smile on your face,
The taste is like the richest chocolate.
It smells like lavender in the air.
You feel as bouncy as a spring,
As playful as a puppy.
As clever as a scientist and as creative
As an inventor.
I love happiness.

Melissa Perrin (10)
Green Park Community Primary & Nursery School, Maghull

Happiness

Happiness is yellow like the sparkling sun
It sounds like children having lots of fun
Happiness tastes like ice cream on a hot day
And the smell is like a bunch of colourful flowers
It reminds me of the exciting story - Talking Showers
Happiness looks like a big smile on someone's face and
It feels like a long silk lace.

Emily McLean (9)
Green Park Community Primary & Nursery School, Maghull

Love!

Love is red, like a soggy tube of lipstick.
It sounds like a beautiful soothing love song
that hums through the room.
It tastes like a gorgeous sloppy kiss
that soothes your nerves.
It looks like a sweet love heart that drifts through
the air when you're looking up at the clouds.
It smells like a beautiful, sweet, freshly baked box of chocolates
when made, especially from Thorntons.
It feels like that giant hug you get off your husband, which you've been
waiting for all day, after coming home from a hard day's work.
Love reminds me of a great friendship that goes on
and gets better after years to come.

Jack McGregor (10)
Green Park Community Primary & Nursery School, Maghull

Fun

Fun is as gold as a huge pot of shiny gold and sparkles
in the light.
It tastes like a crisp of delight going all around your body
which makes you smile.
The sound of laughter threads through the air and the sound
of the sea fills you with delight.
Fun smells of lovely red, crunchy strawberries, which have
just been picked from a big bush.
As I look around, all I can see is people giggling and smiling,
but having fun!
The word fun, reminds me of a sweet yellow sun
and the clouds spell . . . fun!

Kyle Lewis (10)
Green Park Community Primary & Nursery School, Maghull

Love

Love is red like a heart pumping blood,
Love sounds like a heart pumping hard in
someone's body but it's much more than that.
Love tastes like sweet and sour chicken in a sweet sauce,
and it's sizzling in the pan.
Love smells like petals growing on a rose that's
used to give to girls.
Love looks like a flower, waving in the distance
with petals drifting in the air.
Love feels like a cuddle from people who are
close by you.
Love reminds me of a fire, burning softly at midnight
while stars are flying past.

Michael Johnson (10)
Green Park Community Primary & Nursery School, Maghull

Silence

Silence is white, like the snowflakes falling
                    from the winter sky,
It sounds like mice creeping across
                    the floor,
Silence tastes like chocolate melting
                    in your mouth.
It smells like air drifting through
                    your nose.
It looks like people having a snooze
                    in their chairs.
Silence feels like ice melting
                    in your hands,
It reminds you of beautiful children, sleeping
                    in their snugly beds.

Milly Brady (9)
Green Park Community Primary & Nursery School, Maghull

Frustration

Frustration is black, like the darkness at night,
It tastes like an explosion in your hands.
You can't see frustration, but you can see it on
Someone else.
It sounds like someone is controlling you.
It smells like air rushing swiftly past your nose.
It feels like a smash and a crash.
It reminds me of not getting my own way!

Connor Boswarva (10)
Green Park Community Primary & Nursery School, Maghull

Happiness

Happiness is blue like a tear of happiness,
It sounds like my friends laughing happily.
It tastes like nothing you have ever tasted before,
It smells like a sweet scent, like candyfloss.
It looks like everyone smiling and having fun.
It feels that something warm in my hand, that is soft.
It reminds me of my best friend Ellie and my family.

Emma Bullen (9)
Green Park Community Primary & Nursery School, Maghull

Silence

Silence is blue like the glistening blue sea,
                  it also sparkles like glitter,
It breaks when you say it, like the sound of water
                  crashing on the ground.
Silence is beautiful, like the taste of plain
                  white water.
It smells like the sweet smell of sugar and honey
                  sprinkled over a soft sponge cake.
Silence reminds me of my new baby brother
                  sleeping silently.
It feels like a soft fluffy cloud floating through
                  the sky.
Silence, it's invisible to see but you know
                  when it's around.

Emily Bateman (10)
Green Park Community Primary & Nursery School, Maghull

Happiness

Happiness is like a blue sea, shining in my eyes,
It sounds like birds singing sweet songs like a piano player,
It tastes like a fresh red rosy apple,
It is like a rainbow flag.
It feels like shouting, 'Wake up world!'
It reminds me of love.

Matthew Albertina (10)
Green Park Community Primary & Nursery School, Maghull

Darkness

Darkness is as black as the darkest mist,
It sounds like an abandoned, lifeless town
Not been touched for years on end.
It tastes like space - nothing to taste and nothing to see
But the stars are so very far away.
It smells like none other but the unstable wind,
But it looks like the deepest night sky of the eclipse,
It feels like none other but the midnight sky.

Sam Albanese (10)
Green Park Community Primary & Nursery School, Maghull

Love

Love is red like a single red rose,
The sound of love is unbelievable, it is the nicest thing
You will ever hear.
Love tastes as sweet as a crunchy red apple,
It smells like fresh strawberries in fresh cream.
Love can look like anything you want it to look like.
Love reminds me of being happy with someone forever.

Holly Hunter (10)
Green Park Community Primary & Nursery School, Maghull

Happiness

Happiness is as yellow as a bright summer's day,
It sounds like the bluebirds singing on top of the clear blue sky
on the hot crowded beaches.
The taste is like candyfloss from an amazing shop with lots
of different things for everyone.
I love the smell of freshly cut grass with lots of different smells
coming up from it.
I can also smell the scent of red roses blooming with
everyone admiring them.
It looks like everyone is enjoying themselves, some with a picnic
some ready to go to posh restaurants.
It feels as if I'm in Heaven with all of my friends and family.
It reminds me of everyone having a good time and it is as if
a giant teddy comes and gives me a big hug.

Sian Williams (9)
Green Park Community Primary & Nursery School, Maghull

Laughter

Laughter is bright pink, like big fluffy candyfloss,
Laughter sizzles like the sweet smell of buttercups.
It tastes as smooth as milky chocolate.
The sound is like a pumping heart.
Laughter looks like the glistening sun
And feels the same as a soft cuddly rabbit.
It reminds me of a colourful rainbow.
Laughter . . . laughter is sweet!

Brooke Whittle (10)
Green Park Community Primary & Nursery School, Maghull

Happiness

Happiness is orange like a log blazing on the hot, hot fire,
It sounds like hyenas laughing in the sweet strong wind.
It tastes like KFC's popcorn chicken.
It smells like fresh air and newly cut grass.
It looks like a big crowd of people, laughing.

George Walsh (9)
Green Park Community Primary & Nursery School, Maghull

The Tudor House

The Tudor house is full of surprises
Oak chests
Priest's holes
Creaking floorboards.

The Tudor house is full of feather pens
Secret rooms
Ancient artefacts
Cracked windows.

The Tudor house is full of boy's turning spits
Hazelnuts
Tasty chicken.

The Tudor house is full of ghosts
Ghostly laughter
Little pitter-patter of ghostly feet!

Isabel Warren (7)
Higham St John's CE (Controlled) Primary School, Higham

The Tudor House

The Tudor house is full of surprises
Secret priest holes
Big oak chests
And broken windows.

The Tudor house is full of ghosts
The tiptoe of shadows
The creak of the floorboards
The creak of the cradle.

The Tudor house is full of excitement
Double doors and bedbugs.
Four-poster beds and . . .
Babies that can't move in swaddling clothes!

Joel Punchard (9)
Higham St John's CE (Controlled) Primary School, Higham

The Tudor House

The Tudor house is full of surprises . . .
The priest hole is a place for the priests to hide away,
Catholics being attacked by Protestants
Queen Elizabeth wanting her own way!

The Tudor house is full of secret rooms and lots of windows,
They did not have pens or pencils, like we do now.
Feather pens, dipped in ink
But made big ink blobs, if you're not careful.

The Tudor house is full of excitement
A Tudor girl played hide-and-seek,
She went and hid in one of the chests
And suffocated, because the chest lid was hard to open
They were too late to save her.

Molly Louise Barnes (8)
Higham St John's CE (Controlled) Primary School, Higham

The Tudor House

The Tudor house is full of ghosts
Tingly laughter
Loud tiptoeing
A baby's cradle rocks all by itself.

The Tudor house is full of spookiness
Creaky floorboards
Ghosts flying past that make sounds like *Swoosh!*
People moaning in the priest hole in the wall.

The Tudor house is full of exciting secret rooms,
Feather pens
Finding out a ghost story
And lots more things.

Alex Boland (8)
Higham St John's CE (Controlled) Primary School, Higham

The Tudor House

The Tudor house is full of rooms
Rooms with food,
Rooms with games,
Rooms with biting bedbugs.

The Tudor house is full of ghosts,
Ghosts filled with laughter,
Ghosts playing games,
Ghosts pinching food.

The Tudor house is full of priest holes,
Priest holes, dark and small,
Priest holes up the chimney,
Priest holes, behind walls.

The Tudor house is full of artefacts,
Like quills and ink,
Big oak chests,
Carved tables.

Harry Jackson-Smith (7)
Higham St John's CE (Controlled) Primary School, Higham

The Tudor House

The Tudor house is full of excitement
Secret rooms everywhere.
Priest holes, so people can hide,
Creaking floorboards in each room.

The Tudor house is full of surprises,
Ghosts upstairs, hiding
Ghosts laughing and hiding where you can't see them,
High rooms at the top of the house.

The Tudor house is full of shocks
Ancient artefacts in different places.
Quills for people to write with
Red wax to make sure the letters won't get wet.

Ben Cox
Higham St John's CE (Controlled) Primary School, Higham

The Tudor House

The Tudor house is full of surprises,
At night, you can hear noises.
You can hear a cradle rocking, all by itself,
And the candlelight flickers on and off
In the night, at the Tudor house.

Callam Barnes (8)
Higham St John's CE (Controlled) Primary School, Higham

The Tudor House

The Tudor house is full of surprises
Secret rooms
Dark priest holes
Loud creaking floorboards.

The Tudor house is full of spookiness
The babies' cradles, creaking at night
Ghostly laughter
Freaky ghostly footprints.

The Tudor house is full of excitement
Feather pens
Wonderful rooms
Ancient antiques
And everything else.

Daniel Shapland (8)
Higham St John's CE (Controlled) Primary School, Higham

The Tudor House

The Tudor house is full of surprises,
Creaking floorboards and secret rooms awaited.

The Tudor house has a girl who was playing hide-and-seek,
She hid in a chest, she couldn't lift the lid
So she had suffocated when they found her.

The Tudor house kitchen had a cauldron,
The brown bread was put on a trencher,
We did bows and curtsies.

Kezia Brown (8)
Higham St John's CE (Controlled) Primary School, Higham

The Tudor House

The Tudor house is full of surprises,
It has secret rooms,
At night there are spooky noises.

The Tudor house is full of artefacts,
Quills with the paper beside them,
Diamond shapes in the windows.

Andrew Danson (8)
Higham St John's CE (Controlled) Primary School, Higham

The Tudor House

The Tudor house is full of surprises
Creaking floorboards and lots of noises
Ghostly laughter and tiptoeing on the ground.

The Tudor house is full of rooms
Priest holes
Bedrooms and
Art galleries.

The Tudor house is full of excitement
Ancient artefacts
Oil paintings
Animals hung on the roof in the kitchen
For a hundred years.

Poppie Brogan (8)
Higham St John's CE (Controlled) Primary School, Higham

The Tudor House

The Tudor house is full of surprises,
Secret rooms
Big oak chests
Secret priest holes.

The Tudor house is full of ghosts
Little laughter.
Tiptoeing feet and
Ghostly sounds.

The Tudor house kitchen
Had a cauldron which they cooked their food in,
They had a trencher that they served their food on.
The girls curtsied and the boys bowed.

Olivia Forrest (8)
Higham St John's CE (Controlled) Primary School, Higham

The Tudor House

The Tudor house is full of surprises,
Like secret rooms, creative paintings and broken windows.

The Tudor house is full of ancient antiques like big oak chests,
Strong wooden violas and a spit made out of iron.

The Tudor house is full of rooms
Spooky ones, dangerous ones and ones that are falling apart.

The Tudor house is full of darkness
Dark secret hiding places, darkness around the room
And darkness shocking your body, making you shake.

Bethany Gregson (8)
Higham St John's CE (Controlled) Primary School, Higham

The Tudor House

The Tudor house is full of excitement
Secret rooms everywhere
Ghostly laughter when you don't expect it
Feather pens to write with.

The Tudor house is full of rooms
Long galleries for men and ladies
Kitchen with lots of food
Priest holes for people to hide in.

The Tudor house is full of spookiness
Moving cradles at night
Creaking floorboards in every hallway
Ghosts whispering in every room.

Connor Quinn (8)
Higham St John's CE (Controlled) Primary School, Higham

The Tudor House

The Tudor house is full of
Secret priest holes and creaky floorboards.
The Tudor house is full of ghosts,
At night, you hear noises,
In the morning, it all goes quiet.

The Tudor house is full of spooky rooms
And old chests full of Tudor clothes.
To get in you need to push the big doors
Guarded by lions above the pillars.

Jacob Ratcliffe (7)
Higham St John's CE (Controlled) Primary School, Higham

The Tudor House

The Tudor house is full of surprises
Like creaking floorboards,
And a big oak chest in the dark.

The Tudor house is full of ghosts,
Spooky pictures, watching you
And laughing in the night.
A feather pen writing by itself!

The Tudor house is full of rooms,
The priest hole behind the walls.
Secret rooms all around.

Cameron Walby (8)
Higham St John's CE (Controlled) Primary School, Higham

The Tudor House

The Tudor house is full of excitement
Like priest holes and artefacts,
Creaky floorboards,
Shadows flying across the window sill
And ghosts, whispering.

The Tudor house is full of surprises like
Thunder and lightning struck across the window side,
Ghosts and ghostly noises.
Moving objects.

The Tudor house is full of artefacts like vases
And ornaments
And moving objects.

Jake McNair
Higham St John's CE (Controlled) Primary School, Higham

The Tudor House

The Tudor house is full of surprises,
Hidden priest holes in the walls
Red wax to close letters
Quills, to write with ink.

The Tudor house is full of spooks
True ghost stories
Doors banging
Little girls laughing.

The Tudor house is full of entertainment
Music playing
Curtseying and bowing
Having a joyful time.

Emily Pickup (8)
Higham St John's CE (Controlled) Primary School, Higham

The Tudor House

The Tudor house is full of secret rooms,
The big creaking door when you open it.
The big oak chests creak when you open them,
The shadows fly across the window ledge.

The Tudor house is full of scary ghosts!
The thunder and lightning strikes across your window.
The feather pens are used for writing,
The curtain blows when someone comes flying past!
The cauldron had fire underneath it.
The heavy rain, coming faster, onto the window.
A long time ago, a girl was playing hide-and-seek and
She hid in a chest and the lid was too heavy.
She couldn't lift it up and when they found her,
She was dead!

Ben Jenkinson (8)
Higham St John's CE (Controlled) Primary School, Higham

The Tudor House

The Tudor house is full of surprises
Creaking floors
Freaky staircase
Priest holes.

The Tudor house is full of ancient artefacts
Feather pens
Inks and scrolls
Candles with bees' wax.

The Tudor house is full of ghosts
Ghastly giggles
Tiptoes all over the creepy floors,
The sound of the little girl ghost.

Victoria Parr (9)
Higham St John's CE (Controlled) Primary School, Higham

The Tudor House

The Tudor house is full of surprises
And interesting pictures and secret
Priests' holes and rooms.

The Tudor house is full of ghosts and
Children laughing and doors banging.

The Tudor house is full of antiques
And big oak chests.

The Tudor house is full of entertainment
There's fabulous music and a giant recorder.

Jenny Plunkett (8)
Higham St John's CE (Controlled) Primary School, Higham

The Tudor House

The Tudor house is full of surprises
Creaky doors and spooky holes
Big cracks in Tudor floors.

The Tudor house is full of floors
All you see is doors and doors
And there's also slippery floorboards.

The Tudor house is haunted by ghosts
Exploring different rooms
And scaring different faces.

Bradley Jones (8)
Higham St John's CE (Controlled) Primary School, Higham

The Tudor House

The Tudor house is full of surprises
Letters sealed with red wax
Spooky noises at night
Ghosts tiptoeing around the house.
The Tudor house is full of secrets
A little girl locked up in a chest
Shouting, *'Help, help!'*
But nobody found her.

Thomas Stinchon (8)
Higham St John's CE (Controlled) Primary School, Higham

The Tudor House

The Tudor house is full of surprises,
Like secret rooms, dusty creaking floorboards.
Be prepared to be amused by the priest hole
And the big oak chests.
You will see ancient antiques with a lot of money.

The Tudor house is full of rooms,
Long galleries where ghosts dance
Up and down all night.
Kitchen fires blazing on and off by itself
All day but at night as well.

The Tudor house is full of secrets
Like pictures watching over you.
Ghosts laughing, playing behind your back
So you'd better watch your back!

Ryan Moir (8)
Higham St John's CE (Controlled) Primary School, Higham

The Tudor House

The Tudor house is full of surprises,
Creaking floorboards and doors.
Big empty rooms with big oak chests
And spooky noises.

The Tudor house is full of spooky true stories being told
And ghosts have been seen at night,
The baby's cradle has been seen rocking by itself at night
It might have been a ghost!

The Tudor house is full of spooks and noises,
A Tudor girl died at the house, and now you can hear
Her laughing and tiptoeing around the house.

The Tudor house is full of entertainment
They love acting and dancing and playing.

Simra Ud-Din (8)
Higham St John's CE (Controlled) Primary School, Higham

The Tudor House Is Full Of Ghosts

With creaking floorboards and big oak chests,
Ghostly laughter and little footsteps with pictures
That follow you up the stairs
The baby's cradle rocking by itself.

The Tudor house is full of ancient things
With big beds and priest holes and big cupboards
With feather pens and sealed up letters
And carved out walls with big chandeliers.

The Tudor house is full of rooms
With secret room and the spit in the kitchen
And the art room with lots of great things
And the long gallery where they would play music and games.

Georgia Mackay
Higham St John's CE (Controlled) Primary School, Higham

My Favourite Things

Pets

Pets make you happy,
You can play with them
Pets are playful
They know if you're sick,
Pets always like to play.
Some you can ride or walk with them,
Pets watch you all the time,
Some keep you safe, like the blind.

Stars:

We are a ball of fire,
Heating gas all the time.
We poison anyone who comes,
We sparkle in the night.
We are shooting stars across the midnight sky.

Teddy bears:

Teddy bears are soft,
You can cuddle up to them,
Teddy bears are colourful,
You can take them to bed,
You can take teddy bears for picnics.

Hayley Sarah Roberts (11)
Maryport CE Junior School, Maryport

Darkness

Darkness creeps round every corner,
The sky has twinkling stars,
Silence has descended on us,
The night has finally arrived.

Darkness; black, silent and cold,
Moonlight shining in the darkness,
Not a sound can be heard,
The night has finally arrived.

Darkness plunges through the town,
It creeps through windows and doors,
Not a creature can be seen,
The night has finally arrived.

Hannah Pattinson (11)
Maryport CE Junior School, Maryport

Darkness

I can darken a room that is full of light,
I can even give grown-ups an awful fright.
At night I can tiptoe around the house
Without waking a single small mouse.

I can slip under any door, into any room,
I can even get in the cupboard to find a broom.
At night I give small children a fright,
If I'm not there, children wouldn't sleep at night.

Heather-Leigh Fox (11)
Maryport CE Junior School, Maryport

Rain

I can pitter-patter on windowpanes,

I can trickle along the drains.

When I am in a hurry,
I rush from the sky.

When I cry, I flood your town,
So watch out!

When it is windy,
I can be seen running along.

Ashton Hunton (10)
Maryport CE Junior School, Maryport

The Sun

The sunlight shines in different directions,
I can burn through grass
Like a mouse cutting through the grass.
The beams are streamlined
Across the sky.
They can make a shadow
And blind you.

Thomas Graham (11)
Maryport CE Junior School, Maryport

My Best Friend

My best friend is amazing
But he's just mine!
We share our lemon drops together,
We mix our drinks,
We are best friends forever.
We have lots of special secrets
Just me and him, no one else,
No, just me and Tim.

Jane Telford (11)
Maryport CE Junior School, Maryport

Dragons

Dragons are fearsome
In all kinds of ways
So all the old folk say

They swallow you up trapped in their tum
The only way to stop them is blind them by the sun

People have seen them flying over the bays
Throwing fire-bombs at cars and trains
To all the locals they are proper pains

The day I die I will always remember,
When reptiles could fly.

Alec Telfer (10)
Maryport CE Junior School, Maryport

Terrifying Teachers

Teachers are just terrifying,
They're always saying
'Stop it!'
One day I feel like saying
'Oh please, just hop it!'

Their faces are just terrifying,
With their ugly looking moustaches,
When they come and talk to you,
Their breath smells of rotten trash.

The worst thing is their glasses,
Really big and round,
I always had a dream
To push them through the ground.

My mum and dad are annoying,
They won't let me skip school,
But when I become rich
All day I'll swim in my pool.

Ellie Tunstall (11)
Maryport CE Junior School, Maryport

A Dog's View Of A Human

A human likes to play video games,
A dog likes to play 'fetch'.
Humans tell us to sit down,
We prefer to stand up.

Humans eat chips and burgers,
Dogs eat dog biscuits,
Humans tell us to be quiet and stop barking,
We prefer to be loud.

Sean Brough (10)
Maryport CE Junior School, Maryport

Snow

A flurry of ice cream, caring and white,
A gentle caress, soft and kind.
Sometimes causing casualties, serious and mild,
Creating snowmen, tall and thin,
Producing snow fights between children, violent and not extreme,
Covering the ground in a blanket, huge and slightly grey.

An explosion of flakes, fluffy and curved,
Inventing a silent surrounding, quiet and undisturbed.
Carefully falling through the night, quickly and slowly,
Making the world look romantic, frosting the ground and icing the air,
Crunch, crunch, go your feet, walking along, loudly and softly.
Melting rapidly when the sun comes out.

Carrie Brogden (11)
Maryport CE Junior School, Maryport

My Hometown

My hometown is where I live,
This is where my heart is.
Living here is such fun,
Chilling out every summer in the sun.

After the sun has disappeared
And the rain is falling down,
The sky turns grey and black,
Puddles form all around the town.

My coastal town by the sea,
Is filled with Roman history.
A lovely museum and fort on the hill,
Many places to visit if the wind has a chill.

One hot summer's night,
I stood on the pier alone
And thought to myself,
This is 'home sweet home'!

Ashlea Hill (11)
Maryport CE Junior School, Maryport

The Rottweiler

I strike fear into everyone's hearts,
I'm big, magnificent and proud.
People will get a fright,
From my fearful bite!
I pull my owner off his feet,
I am one for my own,
I don't go in groups,
For I am the head bully.
I may be stocky,
I may be dim,
But I am the Rottweiler and
I am strong!

Hannah Bethwaite (11)
Maryport CE Junior School, Maryport

The Shiny Coin

There is a coin,
A one pound coin.
It sparkles and glistens in front of me,
I see the past.
One hundred and sixty million years ago,
When dinosaurs ruled the world.

I drop the coin,
The one pound coin.
Knowing my luck, it misses the floor,
It falls down the drain.
Weeping and sobbing.
I want if back.

I need the coin,
The one pound coin.
The one I dropped down the drain,
I feel something in my pocket,
It's the coin!
The one that sparkles and glistens.

Charlie Donaldson (10)
Maryport CE Junior School, Maryport

The Unknown

Speeding out into the endless black,
Flaming meteors are burning up.
Stars are glinting in formation,
Suns exploding into darkness.
Black holes gaping devouring planets,
Multicoloured planets, which may contain life.
The universe is endless.

Adam Wozencroft (11)
Maryport CE Junior School, Maryport

The Dream

Step into a different world,
When you close your eyes
Anything is possible!

You're walking down a ragged path
Towards a violet sea,
With bright green clouds
And a deep scarlet sky.
Anything is possible!

Then you see two eyes
Watching your every step,
You run in panic and hear a voice,
'Wake up! Wake up!'
You open your eyes
Your world is gone.
Never to be seen again!

Emily Ford (11)
Maryport CE Junior School, Maryport

The Snail's Trail

A snail has a trail,
It shines and glistens in the sun.
When you see that trail,
Like a shiny path,
You know the snail has been there,
But when the snail grows old and dies,
You can go back to where it has been
And see the trail,
Of that magnificent snail.
The last memories of it being there.

Hayden Barcock (10)
Maryport CE Junior School, Maryport

Under The Sea

Under the sea
Is dark as can be,
There's plenty of life
For you and me.

The fish are plentiful
Swimming about,
Like an enormous cloud
Floating around.

See the seaweed
Swaying to and fro.
The rainbow fish
Have a beautiful glow.

Crabs and lobsters
Are lazy you know,
But cod and haddock
Are not so slow.

How I'd like to swim
Under the sea,
I know this life
Would be smooth and free.

Under the sea
There's not much to see,
It's too dark and eerie
For you and me.

Callum James Morley (10)
Maryport CE Junior School, Maryport

The Life Of A Shadow

The shadow traps you in a silhouette of gloom,
It creeps up behind you whilst you're not looking.
Your shadow always backs you up,
It overhangs you like lingering smog.

The dark shadow startles you,
It follows you like a constant reminder you're still there,
Its shady shape is in the form of your body,
When the sun goes down, your friend is no longer around.

Antonia Hodgson (11)
Maryport CE Junior School, Maryport

The Silly Young Man

There was a young man from Dundee,
Who dropped his cup of tea
He mopped it all up
Even the cup.
That silly young man from Dundee.

Dylan Renac (10)
Maryport CE Junior School, Maryport

A Young Dog

There was a young dog of Dumbree,
Who drank quite a lot of tea,
He went to the vets
And washed out the pets,
That silly young dog of Dumbree.

Daniel Hutchinson (11)
Maryport CE Junior School, Maryport

The Snake

Slimy, slithery,
poisonous, petrifying,
dangerous devil,
curled up,
furious, fast,
super stripy.
They slowly
sneak up on you
and bite badly.

Lauren Thomas (8)
St Mary's RC Primary & Nursery School, Langley

Paul's Ball

Colourful ball, colourful ball,
It went on the wall,
All the way to Paul
And it was very small.
Paul was very tall,
He only had to walk on the tall wall.
The ball went into the hall.

Paul Navin (7)
St Mary's RC Primary & Nursery School, Langley

Ice Cream

Yummy, scrummy vanilla ice cream,
Soft, sweet, scrumptious,
Crunchy cone,
Chocolate coating.
Mine! Mine! Mine!

Chelsea-Lee Stone (8)
St Mary's RC Primary & Nursery School, Langley

Sabre-Toothed Cat

Big teeth,
Completely carnivorous cat.
Predator, good smeller.
Ginger whiskers,
Stripy cat,
Strange looking bird killer.

Zak Howatson (9)
St Mary's RC Primary & Nursery School, Langley

Sweets

Sweets, they are my favourite treat,
They are my favourite thing to eat.
You need to pay the price,
None of them taste of mice.
I like to eat a lovely sweet!

Nicole Herbert (9)
St Mary's RC Primary & Nursery School, Langley

Animals

Lions have a really big mane,
Rats are tiny but still a pain,
Tigers have massive claws,
Kittens have tiny paws
Snails always leave a trail.

Rachel Stothers (9)
St Mary's RC Primary & Nursery School, Langley

Animals

My cat is really, really fat
He's always lying down on my mat.
He looks like a cheetah,
His friend is called Peter
But sometimes he thinks he's a bat.

Morgan Andrew (8)
St Mary's RC Primary & Nursery School, Langley

Rabbits

Bunnies can be a little tough
Bunnies can be hoppy and rough.
They love it when they're fed
And they can bump their head.
They are full of nice fluffy fluff.

Rysia Freeman (9)
St Mary's RC Primary & Nursery School, Langley

Football!

John Terry smashed his face in mud
I confess that's not very good.
He tried to hit the ball
Missed and hit the wall.
Now his foot is covered in blood.

Shannon Wilks (8)
St Mary's RC Primary & Nursery School, Langley

Chocolate

I ate a nice packet of rice
I got some chocolate, it was nice
I got a chocolate dice
I got a sacrifice
I gobbled some chocolate twice.

Niamh Lomas (8)
St Mary's RC Primary & Nursery School, Langley

Ice Lollies

My ice lollies get really licked
But I don't want them to be kicked
My ice lollies are really nice
I like to take a slice
My ice lollies are really quite thick.

Adam Evans (9)
St Mary's RC Primary & Nursery School, Langley

Friends

Life is tough without many friends
We need them to follow our trends
Our friends keep us happy
Some still wear a nappy
Without them my life would just end!

Hannah Devlin (9)
St Mary's RC Primary & Nursery School, Langley

Football

Where would I be without football,
We always play against the wall.
United make me glad,
While City make me mad.
That's all I can say 'bout football.

James Tudor (9)
St Mary's RC Primary & Nursery School, Langley

Ice Lollies

Lollies are supposed to be licked,
Sometimes they are fat, thin or thick.
If you take a big slice,
It will be very nice,
And then you can chew on the stick!

Jade Taylor (9)
St Mary's RC Primary & Nursery School, Langley

The Great Game!

John Terry scored a great free kick,
Ran to the crowd and gave a flick.
Then ran all the way back,
Ready for the attack.
But they beat them off with a stick.

Thomas Rutter (8)
St Mary's RC Primary & Nursery School, Langley

Aliens

Aliens aren't handsome they're green,
I watch them 'cause they're really mean.
They go to a weird place
To see their ugly face.
'This is not a good film,' said Dean.

Ijeoma Ehigiator (9)
St Mary's RC Primary & Nursery School, Langley

Cars

In my dad's car I had a meal,
While I was sitting in a wheel.
I looked up to the stars
And I saw many cars
It really was very surreal.

Joseph Navin (9)
St Mary's RC Primary & Nursery School, Langley

Brown Bunny

Brown bunny, big teeth,
Perfect pink nose,
Large, long ears.
Tasty apples and carrots to eat.

Lauren McCarthy (8)
St Mary's RC Primary & Nursery School, Langley

T-Rex

Terrifying T-rex rules the land.
Perfectly, powerful predator smells its prey.
Big-headed, bloodthirsty bully with big sharp teeth.

Dominic Fox (8)
St Mary's RC Primary & Nursery School, Langley

Cats

I am a cat,
I am clean and cute and cuddly,
Soft and sweet.
I purr and prowl and have kittens.

Kiana Binns (8)
St Mary's RC Primary & Nursery School, Langley

Funny Fish

I have a fish called Frank,
Who really loves his tank.
Dizzy damp fish
Is a funny, funky fish.
Slow swimmer, star blower
Big bubbles.

Leonie Morrison (9)
St Mary's RC Primary & Nursery School, Langley

Snake

A scaly shedder, super fast,
Frighteningly fierce fangs.
Slithering slower,
Ready to strike.
Friendly frogs
A tasty treat.

Jessica Maloney (9)
St Mary's RC Primary & Nursery School, Langley

Cheeky Fred

Fluffy, floppy Fred,
Cuddly, cute and cheeky,
Brown, black, white and soft,
Sits soundly in his cage.

Ezinne Brown (8)
St Mary's RC Primary & Nursery School, Langley

What Is In The Box?

Is it . . .

A little girl screaming?
A tiny owl hooting?
A spotted cheetah stalking?
A zigzag fish swimming?
A bad bull raging?
A king lion roaring?

We don't know let's look.
It's my Man United shirt!

Joseph Rayner (10)
St Mary's RC Primary & Nursery School, Langley

What Is In The Box?

Is it . . .

A blue dragonfly fluttering?
A little doll sneezing?
A smelly rat scatting?
An old watch crackling?
A small fly flying?
A little owl running?

Let's see -
My golden ring!

Grace Large (9)
St Mary's RC Primary & Nursery School, Langley

What Is In The Box?

A silver shell shivering?
A pink pig praying?
A blue bear barking?
A gold giraffe giggling?
A red reindeer reading?
A colourful cat clinging?

I don't know,
Let's look -
My colourful cat clinging!

Jordanna Cheetham (9)
St Mary's RC Primary & Nursery School, Langley

What Is In The Box?

Is it a small ring shining?
Is it a small snake slithering?
Is it a small dog barking?
Is it a dove flying?
Is it a brown crab scurrying?
Is it a golden bird shining?
Is it an owl hooting?
Is it a shiny fish swimming?
Is it a shining sea whispering?
Is it a beautiful baby talking.

We don't know,
Let's look!

Liam Hall (9)
St Mary's RC Primary & Nursery School, Langley

Going Shopping

Going shopping, going far,
Really need to take the car.
Into the back seat, seatbelt on,
Mother's driving, oh what fun!
Down the street, round the corner,
People walking, funeral mourners.
Slowing down, pelican crossing,
Children skipping, mothers bossing.
Over the bridge, first on the right,
Past the fields, flowers so bright.
Up the lane, farmer ahead,
Taking all the cows home to bed.
Nearly there, what will Mum buy me?
Shoes, jewellery - maybe I'll have to see.

Abbie Rayner (10)
St Mary's RC Primary & Nursery School, Langley

Under The Sea

As I say these words they break into tiny bubbles.
By the way, my name is Grumbles.
They call me that because my tummy always rumbles.

As I go down, down, down,
My feet finally touch the ground.
I start to explore more and more,
What's this? Is it true? Did I just find the very first clue?
I go down into the deep blue even more,
Then I see an open door.

I go inside and glide across the floor
Then the door shuts with a bang.
A seashell rang how can this be?
It says I'm in danger
Because sharks are here to catch me!

How do I escape?
I swim up and up onto the surface,
Then a volleyball hits my face.
I'll look again tomorrow and find the treasure.

I'll have to hurry up,
My pressure is going up.
So good luck to me and good luck to you.
I hope you find the buried treasure
That would be a pleasure.

Courtney Leigh Hodkinson (10)
St Mary's RC Primary & Nursery School, Langley

Fairy Treasure

Fairies fly through windows,
For treasure they need to know,
And they hold on tight,
Just like dynamite.

Then fly on the fairy lane,
To search for a tooth for the wall of fame.
They search for shiny teeth,
They don't care if dirty or clean.

They don't get bracelets
For their teeth return,
In fact the treat they get
Is coins, golden ones of course.

So as you see,
They are both happy
For they both have treats.
See, you get money for teeth.

Amber Hardman (9)
St Mary's RC Primary & Nursery School, Langley

The Silly Cat Comes To Play

Sophie and I were playing one day,
When the silly cat came to play.
He said, 'Why that is no fun, no fun, no fun.
Come outside and play in the sun!'

Then I went and said to the cat,
'We're having fun and that is that!
We don't need to do what you say,
So can you please let us play!'

The cat looked sad and then he said,
'I think I'll have a rest in bed.
I am quite tired anyway,
Sorry to bother you, carry on and play.'

A few minutes later, do you know what we found?
That silly cat, bouncing around!
He was bouncing on Mama's bed,
If she were here, she would have said,

'Oh no, you two, what have you done?
My bed is not for jumping on!'
We would have been in so much trouble
And sent to bed in a hubble.

I got very angry and then I said,
'Get off of Mama's bed!
Go outside, go home!
We just want to be left alone!'

Then the cat said, 'Cheerio,'
And left me and Sophie alone.
We were pleased to be rid of that cat,
We were very pleased, and that is that!

Abigail Flynn (10)
St Mary's RC Primary & Nursery School, Langley

Engineers

Pistons, valves and wheels and gears,
That's the life of engineers.
Thumping, chunking engineers going,
Hissing steam and whistles blowing.

There's not a place I'd rather be,
Than working around machinery.
Listen to that clanking sound,
Watching all the wheels go round and round.

Hayden Fitzpatrick (10)
St Mary's RC Primary & Nursery School, Langley

My Horse Hayley

My horse Hayley is so huge,
My horse Hayley is the best,
My horse Hayley is so clean,
My horse Hayley can beat the rest.

Get up early
We need to go,
Get some breakfast
We're going to the show.

Now we're there you need to eat,
Plait your hair,
Wash you down,
Let's go and see who you need to beat.

Collette Pickering (10)
St Mary's RC Primary & Nursery School, Langley

Swimming

Me and my best friend go swimming.
We go to swimming lessons on Friday.
We have a race and I always keep winning.
The swimming bath floors are so slippery.

In the swimming baths we always play,
It is such fun.
At the end of the day
We always have a chocolate bun.

The next day is Saturday,
That is the day I like to play.
My favourite day is Friday.
My friend has got a baby sister called Fay.

Lana O'Neill (10)
St Mary's RC Primary & Nursery School, Langley

The Match

I'm going to a match,
I've got the best patch.
We want to win,
It's so quiet, you could hear someone drop a pin.
Suddenly the fans are out of their chairs,
Whilst their opponents are pulling out their hair.

Finally it's a goal,
Scored by Graham Poll.
What a goal,
In the net, through the hole.
Now it's the end,
I'm off to meet my friend.

Robert Aylmer (10)
St Mary's RC Primary & Nursery School, Langley

The Cruise Adventure

In Spain, in America,
I am going to have a good adventure.
To Africa, to France,
I would never take a chance.
This is so cool,
I'm acting like a fool.
My room is pink,
Oh, not got time to think.
In Australia, on TV
I really think I've broken my knee.
I find a cat,
It has a hat.
It's in boots,
Its name is Toots.

I see a police boat.
I like their coats.
In Poland, in Germany,
This has been a good journey.
Whales, dolphins, sharks, fish,
I want my first wish.

Lucy Cornford (10)
St Mary's RC Primary & Nursery School, Langley

I Hate My Brother

I hate my brother,
He always puts his programmes on
And hides the remote.

I have my brother,
He always rips up my homework.

I hate my brother,
He takes my mail and hides my money.

I hate my brother,
He scribbles on my favourite magazines.

But after all he is my brother,
And I still love him.

Francesca Slattery (9)
St Mary's RC Primary & Nursery School, Langley

What Is In The Box?

Is it . . .

An old watch ticking?
A buzzy bee buzzing?
A dragonfly whizzing?
A small mouse squeaking
Or a golden belt sparkling?
What could it be?

I don't know,
Let's look and see -
It is a shiny shell.

Hayden Thomas (11)
St Mary's RC Primary & Nursery School, Langley

From A Car
(Based on 'From A Railway Carriage' by Robert Louis Stevenson)

Faster than fairies, faster than witches,
Where are we being taken?
Charging along like troops in a battle,
Through the hills, over the meadows.
All the sights of the hill
Faster and faster I go;
And never again in the wink of my eye,
Other cars go by.

Here is a horse that galloped and galloped
All by himself and gathering others;
Here is a tramp who stands and gazes
And there is a green for stringing daisies.
Children running in the road,
Lumping along with man and load;
Each a glimpse and gone forever.

Emma Wilson (10)
St Mary's RC Primary & Nursery School, Langley

Football

If Mum would let me, if I could
I'd play ball in a heavy flood
I'd play in lots of hay
Or on a Saturday
I like being covered in mud.

Thomas Pluples (9)
St Mary's RC Primary & Nursery School, Langley

Queen

This queen was always really mean
She didn't like to be a team
She really was quite small
But enjoyed a good ball
But she was always really keen.

Charlotte Proctor (8)
St Mary's RC Primary & Nursery School, Langley

People Of My School

I am the nicest girl in school,
I am best in the swimming pool,
I am good at maths,
I have some laughs,
I am good at art,
I must be smart.

I am the bully of the school,
Me and my friends are very cool,
I hate maths,
I never go to the swimming baths,
I really can't draw,
I don't obey the school law.

I am the smallest girl in school,
I can't stand up in the swimming pool,
I think tall people stink
And small kids rule,
I may be small
But inside I'm tall.

So you have met my group of friends
With different silliness and trends,
You have listened to what they had to say,
Maybe you'll hear them again one day.

Jasmin Monaghan (10)
St Mary's RC Primary & Nursery School, Langley

I Have A Dream

I have a dream . . .

To be a professional skier,
Skiing in different parts of countries,
Swooping, gliding, drifting,
Like an eagle diving for its prey,
Like penguins flapping their humongous feet.
It makes me feel so adventurous,
Like a bird twittering loudly,
A swooping, spectacular skier.
Give me the key to my dream!

I have a dream . . .

To make a difference to hunger in Africa.
Living with no food or water,
Disappointed, starving, dying.
Like living people suffering from poverty,
Like living without hope and no air to breathe.
It makes me feel like I need to do something,
Like a prime minister standing up for his country.
Make a difference with food in Africa.

Hannah Shaw (11)
St Vincent's RC Primary School, Penketh

I Have A Dream

I have a dream . . .

That one day I will be a professional show jumper.
Jumping over the fences, winning first place.
Glorious, graceful, gliding
Like a bird flying smoothly over the clouds.
Like a rabbit hopping to its burrow.
It makes me feel proud,
As proud as a fox coming home with its prey.
A professional show jumper
Reminds me that anything is possible.

I have a dream . . .

That one day animal cruelty will be terminated.
Killing animals for money or fun,
Tyrannical, terrible, tragic.
Like war starting for no reason.
Like an ocean full of heartless water.
It makes me feel powerless
Like a flea trapped inside a jar.
Animal cruelty
Reminds me every animal has a life.

Tara Moran (11)
St Vincent's RC Primary School, Penketh

I Have A Dream

I have a dream . . .

That one day starvation will stop.
Leaving people to stay and die is
Disgraceful, evil, terrible.
It's like our bodies being ripped to pieces,
Like our hearts have stopped beating,
Like a pencil's shavings left on the floor.
It makes me feel helpless.
Starvation needs to go!

Jennifer Gibbons (11)
St Vincent's RC Primary School, Penketh

The Ocean

The ocean,
Created by God thousands of years ago,
Glistening, graceful, gleaming
Like a never-ending sink full of water,
Like a blue blob consuming the Earth.
It makes me feel tiny
Like a molecule trapped in a huge room.
The ocean
Reminds us how big the world is.

Ben Baxter (11)
St Vincent's RC Primary School, Penketh

Slaughter Machines

The hunters
They kill defenceless, innocent animals,
Vicious, cruel, cold-hearted.
As red as blood which drips from a lion's mouth
After killing the innocent animal on the savannah grassland.
As dark as a demon creeping up on you from behind
In a dark room at midnight.
Sickens my stomach inside,
And on the outside, I feel like I'm going to explode.

The hunters
Stop the cruelty now!

Zachary Wilde (10)
St Vincent's RC Primary School, Penketh

I Have A Dream

I have a dream . . .

That Old Trafford will be a humungous stadium,
With a roar from the crowd!
Tremendous, spectacular, unbelievable,
Like a man shouting at a child,
Like a lion deafening another animal.
I feel so enraptured.
I'm like a diminutive ant in the whole crowd.
Old Trafford will be a humungous stadium.
Reminds me of how good Man U are.

Aamil Ashraf (10)
St Vincent's RC Primary School, Penketh

I Have A Dream

I have a dream . . .

To be a professional gymnast.
It is a sport for males and females,
Strong, flexible, prepared
Like a spider twisting and turning to make her web,
As flexible as a worm.
It makes me feel I can be myself.
Like a monkey swinging from vine to vine.
To be a professional gymnast
I need to live my dream now!

I have a dream . . .

To feed the poor children in Africa.
More and more die every day.
Poor, ill, hungry,
Like rain falling to the ground,
Like leaves dropping off the tree.
I feel something must be done.
Like one tiny ant standing up for himself
To feed the poor children.
Let my dream begin now!

Emily Purcell (11)
St Vincent's RC Primary School, Penketh

I Have A Dream

I have a dream . . .

To bungee-jump from the sky.
To feel the icy breeze glide across my face.
Twirling, gliding, escaping.
Like an eagle soaring through the sapphire sky.
Like a tornado twisting through a misty heaven.
It makes me feel dizzy that something so big is surrounding me!
Let me start my windy roller coaster to the sky . . .

Charlie English (11)
St Vincent's RC Primary School, Penketh

I Have A Dream

I have a dream . . .

To feed the countless children living (no existing)
In Third World countries.
Like living skeletons walking the hot Earth.
Lives in despair like a living nightmare.
It makes me feel so helpless
Like a tiny insignificant ant.
The countless starving children need feeding now!

Daniel McCormick (11)
St Vincent's RC Primary School, Penketh

The Bully

The bully,
The pressure pusher.
Cruel, spiteful, hurtful.
As wet as a vicious storm
Not leaving you alone.
As sly as a fox hunting for its innocent prey.
Making people cry as they rattle through crowds.
As sad as a baby crying for its mother.
The bully
Needs to stop!

Hannah Rhodes (10)
St Vincent's RC Primary School, Penketh

I Have A Dream

I have a dream . . .

That one day bullying will be stamped out of all schools,
Hurting the feelings of children.
Horrendous, upsetting, terrifying.
Like being stranded on a desert island,
As hurtful as a stab wound.
It makes me feel small and lonely,
Like a bit of dirt on somebody's shoe.
Bullying, it needs to be stamped out now!

Amy Matthews (11)
St Vincent's RC Primary School, Penketh

I Have A Dream

I have a dream . . .

That one day wars will come to an end
And people can live in peace.
Separating soldiers from their families,
Heartbreaking, horrific, horrendous,
Like a bullet piercing my heart,
Like a living nightmare.
It makes me feel useless
Like a precious life going to waste.
One day wars will come to an end.
People are killed.

Meghan Gleave (11)
St Vincent's RC Primary School, Penketh

Help The Majestic Tiger

The magnificent tiger,
Unjustly slaughtered by Man for its beautiful coat.
Amazing, spectacular, out of this world.
As powerful as a muscular male horse fighting with another.
As proud as a peacock opening its feathers to show off
                                                    to an admiring female.
As ferocious as a giant dragon, being confronted by a knight
                                                    in shining armour.
I would be ashamed if I were those poachers.
I'm as furious as the red Devil when people are doing good.

The tiger.
This killing needs to stop!

Claudia Perez (11)
St Vincent's RC Primary School, Penketh

I Have A Dream!

I have a dream . . .

That one day I could be a professional show jumper,
Gliding, gorgeously, graciously.
Like a bird soaring through the sky.
Like a plane taking off.
It makes me feel like a professional.
I dream to be a show jumper,
It inspires me a lot.

Kendell Redmond (11)
St Vincent's RC Primary School, Penketh

Save The Animals!

The hunters!
They kill poor, innocent animals.
Cruel, vicious, cold-hearted.
As dark as the night sky without any moon or star.
As sly as a fox.
It makes me want to lock them up
And save all the scared, frightened animals.
As cruel as all the cruelty put together in the world.
The hunters,
Stop the cruelty now!

Beth Carrington (11)
St Vincent's RC Primary School, Penketh

I Have A Dream!

I have a dream . . .

That war will be stopped,
For it may go on for many years.
Scared, horrified, heartbroken,
Like a football game but the ball a bomb.
Like a living action game.
I feel so emotionless, like I'm in the middle.
Please, let this dream come true!

I have a dream . . .

To help the poor children
Who live in the world in need of help.
Hungry, defenceless, dying, like an underground world.
I feel so useless, like a newborn baby.
The poor children in Africa
In need of help!

Jennifer Campbell (11)
St Vincent's RC Primary School, Penketh

I Had A Dream

I had a dream . . .

That animals were facing extinction.
A fight for every day.
Sad, lonely, afraid.
Disappearing as fast as smoke.
Like a colossal cake losing its flavour.
I felt sad and useless, like a smelly rodent.
Animals facing extinction need saving now!

I had a dream . . .

I was a professional black belt (karate),
The Japanese martial art.
Swift, defensive, powerful, fast as a cheetah.
Like a hidden spider waiting to leap for its prey.
I felt confident and strong,
Like a rhino charging full pelt.
To be a professional black belt
I need training now!

Joseph Ellison (11)
St Vincent's RC Primary School, Penketh

I Have A Dream

I have a dream . . .
To go to amazing countries.
The Eiffel Tower, the wonderful pyramids.
Exciting, expressive, colossal,
Like a marble of fantasy unique in every way.
To go to amazing countries.
Give me the key to my world!

I have a dream . . .

To save the hungry,
The hopeless, starving people.
Hungry, lonely, heartbroken.
I feel so insignificant,
Like a person who no one notices.
To save the poor and hungry,
We need to do it now!

Alex Preston (10)
St Vincent's RC Primary School, Penketh

Things Found In A Fairy's Pocket

A roast dinner that is cooking.
Someone who is singing.
The castle as big as a school.
A fairy's magical wand.
Some magical perfume.
A fairy's kitten.
A fairy's pretty wings.
Some fairy slippers to keep her feet warm.

Charlotte Parry (8)
Sutton Green Primary School, Little Sutton

Ten Things Found In Steve Irwin's Pocket

A cranky croc's growl.
A snake's awesome hiss.
The amazing croc file.
The sound of a dolphin's *eek.*
A mad lion's roar.
A really moody boar.
A claw from a lizard,
And a dog called Sui.
An active wallaby
And an elephant's sound.

Daniel McCabe (9)
Sutton Green Primary School, Little Sutton

Ten Things Found In A Princess' Pocket

A sparkling crown.
The smell of baking cakes.
A heart-shaped locket.
The fancy style of the staircase.
The smell of perfume in her bedroom.
The gold of a bracelet.
A fantastic pink fluffy bed.
The sound of beautiful music.
A princess' beautiful watch.
The smell of beautiful roses.

Victoria Garner (7)
Sutton Green Primary School, Little Sutton

Ten Things Found In A Witch's Pocket

A troll's toe as blown as slop.
A frog's eye as slimy as a fish.
Ripped skin from a troll's back.
Swamp slime as slushy as a smoothie.
A horse's foot as skinless as a worm.
A cat's eye as black as the night.
A dog's leg as ugly as a troll.
Snake's venom as yellow as the sun.
A spell as explosive as dynamite.
A crocodile's tail as dry as rocks.

Philip Jones (9)
Sutton Green Primary School, Little Sutton

Ten Things Found In A Witch's Pocket

A spider as hairy as a bear.
The smell of a dying troll.
A million shiny webs.
The smell of boiling parsnips.
Teeth as pointy as sharp knives.
The noise of a cat growling.
A skeleton rotting away.
A person who has been turned into a frog.
A wand that can do every spell in the world.
A broomstick that flies faster than a rocket.

Imogen Buckley (9)
Sutton Green Primary School, Little Sutton

Ten Things Found In A Pixie's Pocket

A pair of wings as small as an ant.
A crown.
Some lipstick as tall as a giant.
A wand.
Some glittery magic dust.
A purple bag.
Some gloves.
A teardrop.
A heart.
Some love.

Emmy Byrnes (9)
Sutton Green Primary School, Little Sutton

Ten Things Found In A Teacher's Pocket

The softest cookie you have ever felt.
The slimiest coffee you have ever smelt.
The noisiest storm you have ever heard.
The crunchiest peanut you have ever seen.
The smelliest wine you have ever seen.
The ugliest flower you have ever seen.
The biggest vase you have ever seen.
The smallest ruler you have ever seen.,
The widest pen you have ever seen.
The thinnest paper you have ever seen.

Darren Whitehill (8)
Sutton Green Primary School, Little Sutton

Ten Things Found In a Genie's Pocket

Magic slippers, as beautiful as a butterfly.
A sparkle of dust glittering in the pale moonlight.
A magic key that opens every door.
A voice of confidence.
Magic powers as bright as the sun.
The scent of perfume in the air.
A magical, mystical hat.
A spell book as magical as a fairy.
A lantern full of power.
A mystical crystal to keep him alive.

Jessica Doig (8)
Sutton Green Primary School, Little Sutton

Ten Things Found In A Kangaroo's Pocket

A woolly jumper as soft as cotton.
A baby kangaroo jumping about.
Boxing gloves as hard as a skull.
The smallest boxing ring in the world.
A big bouncy jump.
A massive skipping rope as long as a snake.
A towel to dry sweat away.
Big feet as bouncy as a ball.
A tail as flat as the world.
A roaring crowd screaming.

Robbie Rogers (9)
Sutton Green Primary School, Little Sutton

Ten Things Found
In A Baseball Player's Pocket

A bat the size of a plank of wood.
A New York Yankee hat.
A baseball as white as snow.
The crowd cheering.
The burgers sizzling.
The manager shouting.
The smell of hot dogs.
Orange foam fingers waving.
Blue and white baseball shoes.
A yellow jersey like the burning sun.

Owen Rutter (8)
Sutton Green Primary School, Little Sutton

Ten Things Found In A Granny's Pocket

A big toy monkey for her grandson.
Some knitting needles for knitting clothes.
A set of small keys.
A walking stick to help her walk.
Curlers for her blonde curly hair.
Sounds of her tapping knitting needles.
A pot of flowers for her lovely garden.
The smell of a roast dinner.
One smelly old tissue.
Pretty, smelly, blue flowers.

Deanna Fairhurst (9)
Sutton Green Primary School, Little Sutton

Ten Things Found In A Witch's Pocket

A wart as big as a curly fingernail.
A black cat as scary as a ghost.
A hat as pointy as a sword.
A potion as smelly as a blue ogre.
A broomstick as old as the dinosaurs.
A house as creaky as a door.
A toad as slimy as goo.
A big murky cloud full of rain and lightning.
A finger as wrinkled as dead skin.
A box of spells the size of a wardrobe.

Alex Cranston (9)
Sutton Green Primary School, Little Sutton

Ten Things Found In A Fairy's Pocket

A pink wand.
A nice white dress.
A pocket full of golden coins.
A pink necklace.
A pink fluffy jacket.
Some pink shoes.
Some beautiful blonde hair.
Some silvery earrings.
A white sparkling clip.
Some lovely rosy red lips.

Sophie Quinn (8)
Sutton Green Primary School, Little Sutton

Ten Things Found In A Headmaster's Pocket

A long pointy whipping stick.
A very naughty child.
A child's blue toy car.
An evil, cruel, cackling teacher.
A red inky pen.
A loud booming voice.
A thick boring book.
A playground as big as a hungry giant.
A child as wild as a fiery lion.
One big, fat, pointy finger.

Holly Powell (9)
Sutton Green Primary School, Little Sutton

Ten Things Found In A Headmaster's Pocket

A naughty child.
A child's beautifully presented work.
A child who goes wild.
An evil teacher's roar.
A horrible loud noise.
A very sharp pencil.
A boy's colourful painting.
A girl's long skipping rope.
A beautiful piece of handwriting.
A big, long, pointy finger.

Lydia Proctor (9)
Sutton Green Primary School, Little Sutton

Young Writers Information

We hope you have enjoyed reading this book - and that you will continue to enjoy it in the coming years.

If you like reading and writing poetry drop us a line, or give us a call, and we'll send you a free information pack.

Alternatively if you would like to order further copies of this book or any of our other titles, then please give us a call or log onto our website at www.youngwriters.co.uk

**Young Writers Information
Remus House
Coltsfoot Drive
Peterborough
PE2 9JX**

(01733) 890066